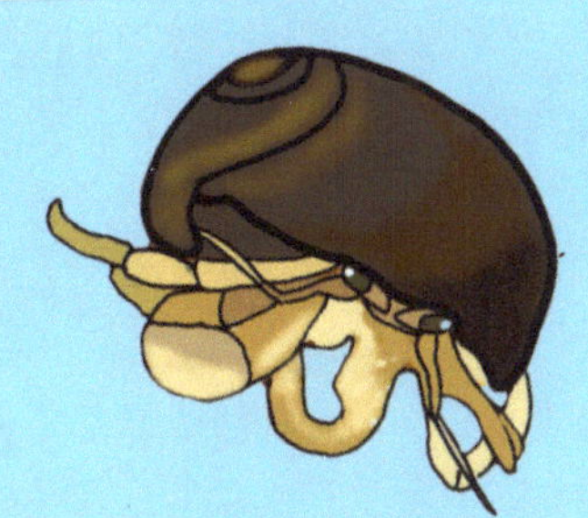

To all the curious kids, may your curiosity never stop.

To the teachers who inspire, may your passion never stop.

Special thanks to Lorrie Martin & Valerie Blansfield

In our world lies a fantastic place to explore, the ocean. It covers a large part of our world and is a fantastic place to explore–offering millions of colorful creatures to meet! Com with me and learn to be friends with the sea and its many wonders.

1.

Welcome to an **estuary**! At the edge of the ocean, lies this partially enclosed body of brackish water. One or more rivers or streams flow into it, and it opens to the sea. Saltwater marshlands protect the land from pounding storm waves and absorb rain waters before they destroy beaches or homes.

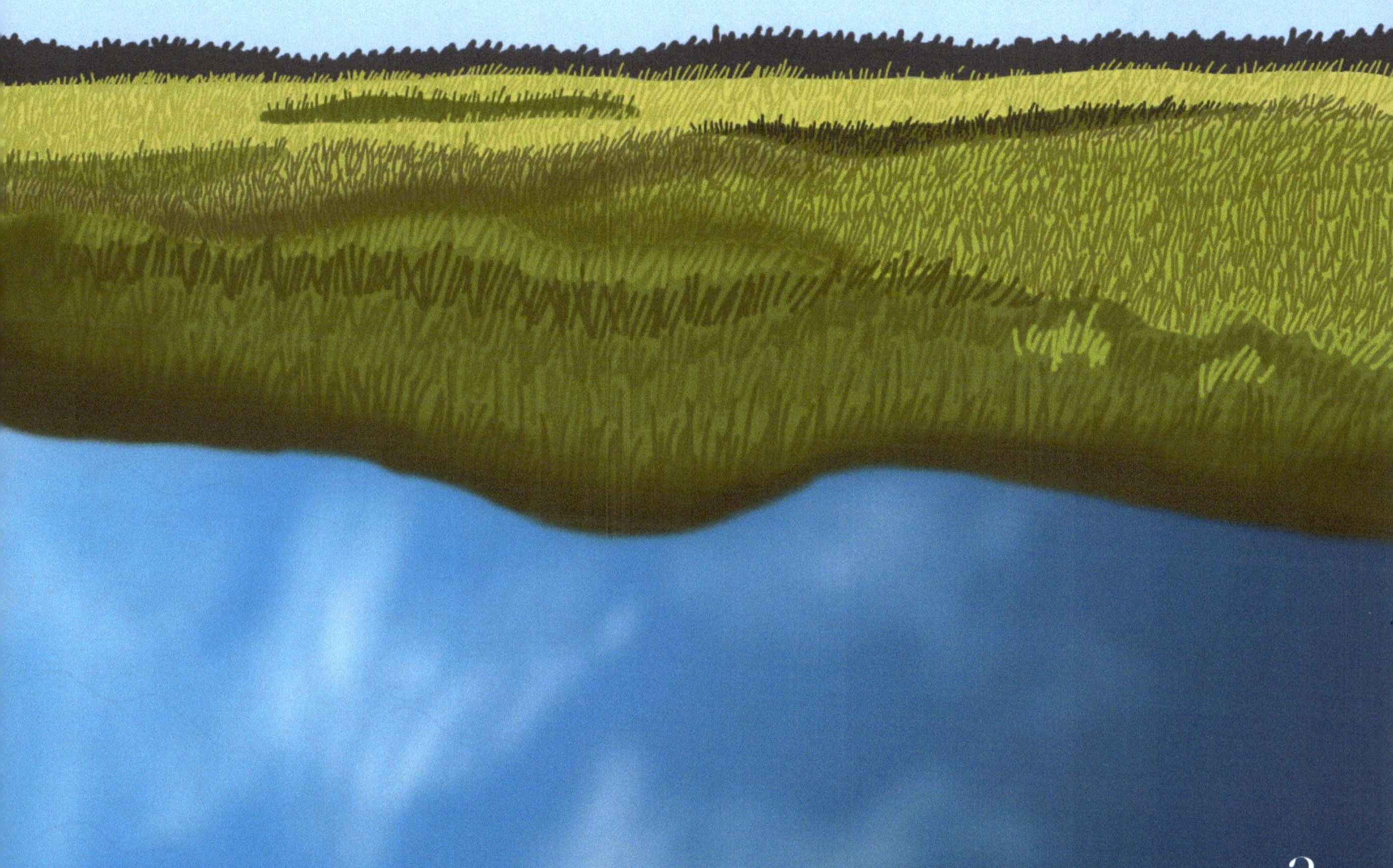

This **fiddler crab** lives in a saltwater marsh, burrowing into a small hole in the sand for protection. Male fiddler crabs invite lady fiddlers into their burrows with a wave of their large claw and eat with the small claw when the water of high tide flows over them. They usually feed on scraps of dead plants and animals.

Have you ever seen this crab where you live?

3.

The **mummichog** and **killifish** can be
found in shallow salt and brackish water.
They are usually small but can grow up to
a few inches in length. Do you see the
periwinkle? It is small and lives on the
rocks. The **hermit crab** can also be found
in shallow water and is always looking for
a slightly larger shell to move into.

Mummichog

Periwinkle

Killifish

Hermit crab

All of these animals can also be found in
brackish waters. The **scallop**, **clam** and
mussel are all different kinds of **bivalves,**
each with two shells. They help keep our
oceans clean as they eat, filtering pollutants
(bad things) out of the water.

How can you help
our ocean?

5.

This is a **moon snail** which can be found in shallow saltwater under the sand. A large foot helps them move under and across the sand as they hunt for food. Their radula can drill a neat round hole into a clam shell through which they reach in and "mop up" their lunch.

Does this moon snail shell look like the moon?

Here we see a **seahorse** blending in with its surroundings, a trick called camouflage. Often found quietly resting in a bed of eelgrass, this unusual fish waits to grab passing plankton. It is amazing that Mom lays her eggs in Dad's pouch, and he "babysits" until the tiny fry are born.

7.

As we bid farewell to the estuary, and plunge into the waves, we'll feel the playful tickle of air bubbles on our faces from our tanks. As we dive deeper, we encounter the magical **coral reef**.

Corals are animals of many sizes, colors and shapes. Inside each individual shell-like cup of a coral lies the polyp or body. Tiny plant-like plankton live inside that polyp body and help make food to share with the coral.

What do you think
          these are?

There are all kinds of turtles, but this is a **sea turtle**! They spend their lives traveling and exploring the amazing ocean world. Many sea turtles grow very large and swim slowly in the deep sea currents.

Where do sea turtles lay their eggs?

10.

Look at this **nudibranch**! Also called sea slugs, they graze on corals, sponges, algae, and more. They use the antennae on their heads to sniff out their food.

Can you name another animal with antennae?

11.

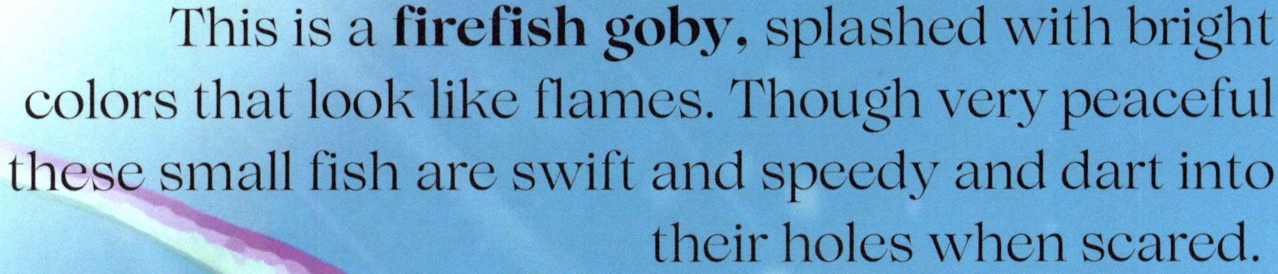

This is a **firefish goby,** splashed with bright colors that look like flames. Though very peaceful these small fish are swift and speedy and dart into their holes when scared.

Why do you think they are so colorful?

12.

The **clownfish** is hiding in a stinging **anemone** for protection. These animals share left over-scraps of food the clownfish has captured. Both benefit by living together-which is called symbiosis.

Beyond the coral reef, there is so much more to discover. Let's dive deeper!

Welcome to the open ocean, home to many amazing creatures. Small animals light up while jellyfish shoot tiny darts to catch food. Sharks and whales cruise the darkened depths!

Can you see the marine snow falling?

Look-a **blacktip reef shark** hunting with a pack of other blacktips on the edge of the reef. Not many people understand how useful these scary sharks are. They catch the slow, the weak and the sick for food, leaving the remaining population of animals healthier as a whole.

Why do most
fish have white
bellies?

15.

This **manta ray** is such a beautiful creature as it glides through the water. Swimming with these gentle giants is entirely safe, as they lack the barbs on their tails that stingrays have.

How big do you think this manta ray is?

This **pufferfish** is swimming through the corals searching for most anything to eat...crabs, shrimp, sponges, worms. It can be ready in a flash to scare off a predator by puffing up like a ball with spines!

How does this
fish puff up?

17.

Do you see these colorful sparkles? This is
a **comb jelly** producing light known as
bioluminescence.

Do you think
they sting?

This fragile filter feeder strains
the water to pick out its food.
Let's dive deeper, where there is
no more light!

18.

Welcome to the deep, a cold, dark region of the sea where sunlight never reaches. Jump in an **ROV** (remotely operated vehicle) to explore where very few people have ever been.

Have you ever seen a **dumbo octopus?** Fins stick out of their head like ears and allow them to navigate, move in currents and even hover. Do you see those big eyes which let them see better in the deep darkness?

Can you believe that this
sea angel is actually a
swimming snail! They
have no shell and can
swim using the "foot".

How do you think they
communicate in the
dark?

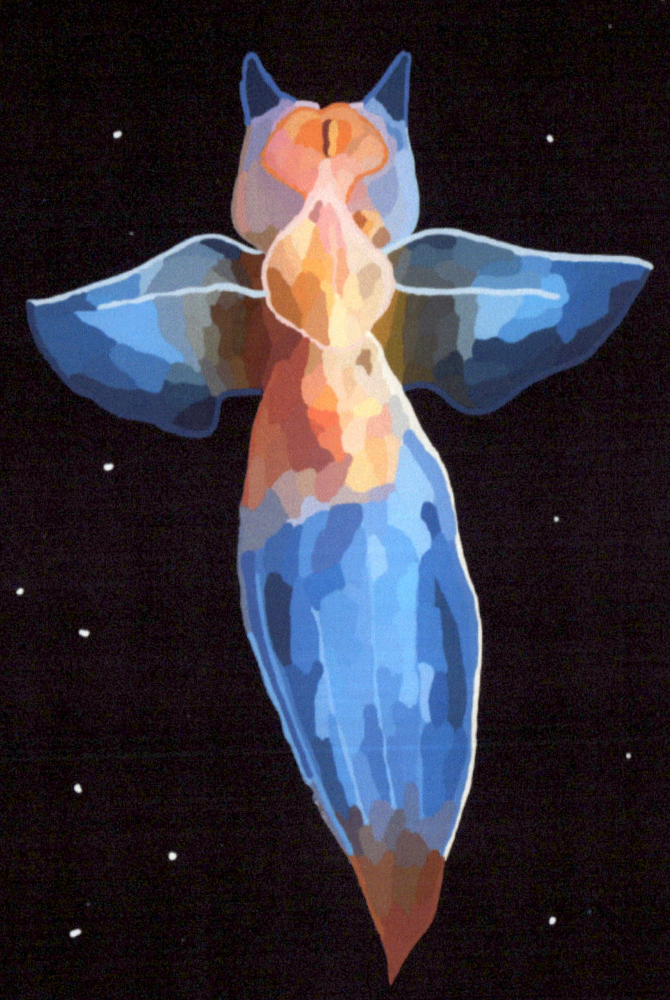

21.

The **nautilus** has been on Earth for over 480 million years! When danger is near, they can close up their shell using a leathery hood or shoot away using jet propulsion.

23.

This is a **blue whale**. It is the largest animal that has ever lived on earth and yet strains out tiny shrimp like krill for its food. This whale can be as long as three school buses and can live up to ninety years old.

Glossary

Invasive Species– A species that came from another environment to a new one, where it doesn't belong.

Brackish Water– Both salt and fresh water.

Camouflage– An animals ability to blend in with its surroundings using different tactics like fur color, or leaf like shape.

Algae– A plant like organism that lives in mostly water.

Migration– Seasonal movement of animals.

Bioluminescence– Animals produce light with their body.

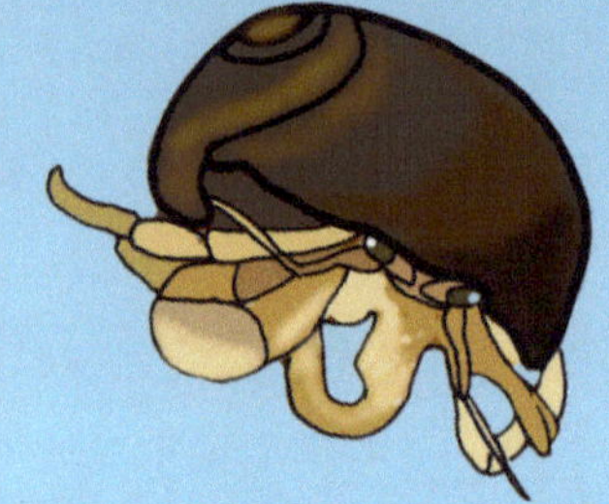

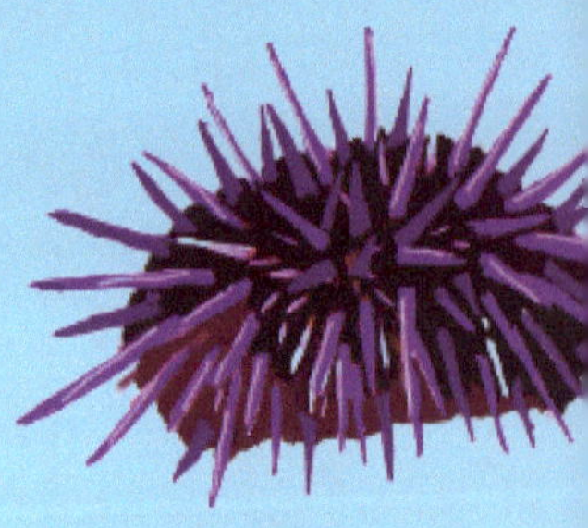

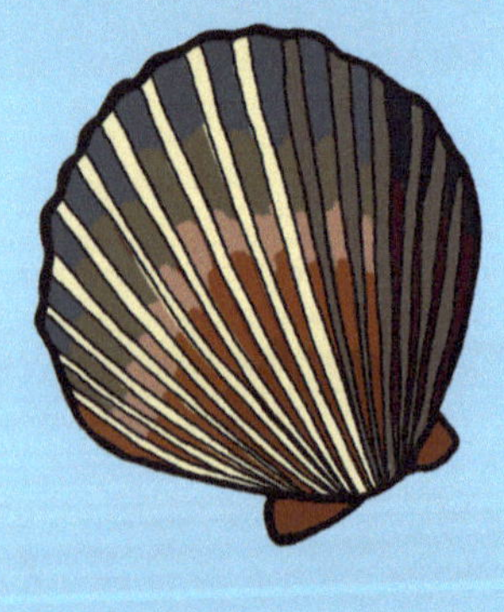

After discovering all
these fascinating ocean
creatures, what kinds of
animals do you hope to
meet at your nearby
seashore?